FastPrayGive

Ending world hunger by the means of grace

Andy Morris

Copyright © 2019 by WesleyMen, INC

All Rights Reserved. No part of this work may be reproduced or transmitted in any form or by any means, electronic or mechanical, including photocopying and recording, or by any information storage or retrieval system, except as may be expressly permitted by the 1976 Copyright Act or in writing from the publisher. Request for permission can be addressed to: WesleyMen, Inc. 3701 Hillsboro Pike, Nashville, TN 37215, or emailed to info@wesleymen.org.

Use of Scripture

Scripture used in this publication is from the Common English Bible (CEB) or the New Revised Standard Version (NRSV) unless otherwise noted.

New Revised Standard Version of the Bible. Division of Christian Education of the National Council of the Churches of Christ in the United States of America, Copyright 1989

The Common English Bible. The Common English Bible, Nashville, TN USA, Copyright 2011.

Chronic malnourishment affects 821 million people in our world today. We grow enough food for everyone. Ours is the first generation on our planet that can end this horrific and intolerable situation. When we involve God and practice means of Grace to align our lives and resources we can deliver compassion and justice to help those persons in need.

The World Methodist Council passed a resolution in 2011 calling the people known as Methodist to Fast one meal per week, Pray during that time for world hunger, and Give to those in need. This became a global initiative of the World Fellowship of Methodist and Uniting Church Men and as a result, launched FastPrayGive.org

This small group study is a resource to aid you in joining this grassroots discipleship movement.

Andy Morris
andymorris@wesleymen.org

Author's Note

This work could not have been completed without the help of Dr. Cosby Stone, Jr. who was my first editor and by all intents and purposes my co-author, because he read it and offered suggestions before anyone else took a peek. A special recognition should be made for the help of Rev. Richard Vance whom was my second line of editing, and he guided me around potholes and, in some cases, craters to avoid. His experience in ministry has been invaluable. Writing this has been slow, but without the encouragement and support from my organizational leader Rev. Steve Hickle: I'd still be in drafts. His encouragement, "Onward!" has been indispensable. Without Rev. Ray Buchanan and Larry Malone getting this kicked off by declaring hunger intolerable and demanding that the people called Methodist do something about it, I would still be languishing in a cubicle. Thank you.

Many other people need to be thanked, and you know who you are, and you are way too humble to be looking for your name at the beginning of this tiny small group study guidebook.

Contents

Use of Scripture ii
Author's Note iv
Foreword 1
Introduction 3
   The Wesley Quadrilateral 7
   Goals to be achieved by this study 8
Chapter 1: That's a lot of Grace 10
   The Description and Definition of Grace 10
   What is grace to the hungry? 11
   Grace in the larger context 13
   Means of Grace 14
      Reflection Questions 16
      Quadrilateralize 16
Chapter 2: The Perception of Hunger 17
   Let's talk about the problem 18
   Let's talk about size 21
   Let's talk about Hope 23
      Reflection Questions 24
      Quadrilateralize 24
Chapter 3: Defeating Guilt and Cynicism 25
   Guilt and Shame 26
   Cynicism 29
      Reflection Questions 34
      Quadrilateralize 34
Chapter 4: Behavior Change 36
   Preparations 39
   Prayer 39
   Fasting 41
      Fasting Suggestions 43
   Giving 42
      Reflection Questions 44
      Quadrilateralize 44
Chapter 5: Casting a Vision 46
   The Change 49
   The Engagement Dichotomy 50
   What do I see? 53
      Reflection Questions 55
      Quadrilateralize 55

Foreword

JOHN WESLEY HAS LONG BEEN one of my role models. From the beginning of his ministry, Wesley understood that there can be no separation between holiness and good works. The two are of one piece. And it is that understanding that is at the heart of this important work by Andy Morris and the FastPrayGive movement.

Wesley believed in a life of good works, service and witness as the proper expression of Christian love and obedience. The three were to be expected of all believers. Like Wesley, I believe that Christians can and should, through God's grace, effectively improve themselves and their world.

According to Wesley, faith does not excuse one from good works. But, in the same breath, he also insisted there can be no good works without faith. Love doesn't release us from the law, but actually fulfills it through constraining us to be obedient.

In one sermon, entitled "Upon Our Lord's Sermon on the Mount: Discourse Four," Wesley spells out his understanding of the necessity of good works like this:

> *1. Whether they will finally be lost or saved, you are expressly commanded to feed the hungry, and clothe the naked. If you can, and do not, whatever becomes of them, you shall go away into everlasting fire. 2. Though it is God that changes hearts, yet he generally doeth it by man. It is our part to do all that in us lies, as diligently as if we could change them ourselves, and then to leave the event to him. 3. God, in answer to their prayers, builds up his children by each other in every good gift; nourishing and strengthening the whole "body by that which every joint supplied."*

Foreword

For Wesley, "faith, holiness and good works" were the roots, the tree and the fruit. They could not be separated. It is the understanding that forms the power behind FastPrayGive.

I have walked alongside the world's poor and hungry for over 40 years. I know that we can end the scourge of hunger in our lifetime. Our generation is the first generation in the history of the world that has the power and the will to eradicate hunger forever. And this study is one important tool that can help people of faith make it happen.

I have a vision of a world without hunger. What I want more than anything else is for that vision to become a reality in my lifetime. In all the years I have known and worked with Andy Morris, he has demonstrated the same vision and same passion for the "least of these among us."

Now, he has given the Church a wonderful gift. Allow this study to open yourself to the cries of the hungry. Use this study to move you to the prayer for those whose need is the greatest. Fill yourself with the power of the Holy Spirit through times of fasting. And then give generously to brothers and sisters you will never meet, but whose very lives are in your hands.

This small booklet is a tool. And like any tool, it is only effective when used. And that is my prayer for you. That you would read these words, that you would use this study as directed, and that you would allow the Holy Spirit to use you in a powerful way to become a leader in ending hunger in our lifetime.

Ray Buchanan, Founder

Society of St. Andrew
Rise Against Hunger

Introduction

¹⁶Jesus said to them, "They need not go away; you give them something to eat."
Matthew 14:16

³⁷But he answered them, "You give them something to eat."
Mark 6:37a

¹³But he said to them, "You give them something to eat."
Luke 9:13a

"You give them something to eat." This is a mandate present in the synoptic gospels of Matthew, Mark, and Luke, often called the story of how "Jesus Feeds the Multitude." Read the entire chapters surrounding these quotes, and you will pick up on how Jesus leads not by mandate, but by example.

The crowd following Jesus in this story has stayed close. Those followers are seeking to hear His words, see His face, and observe His example. Doing so has stretched their resources, and they are hungry, no longer able to pay attention as their stomachs are growling at the end of the day. **Jesus has compassion on them**, and He tells his disciples to do something about it. "You give them something to eat," He says. We, as Jesus' disciples, must understand Christ's compassionate edict and act in response to hungry people. We are to feed the hungry.

Danish Priest and author Henri Nouwen says of compassion, "Compassion challenges us to cry out with those in misery, to mourn with those who are lonely, to weep with those in tears. Compassion

Introduction

requires us to be weak with the weak, vulnerable with the vulnerable, and powerless with the powerless. Compassion means full immersion in the condition of being human." This is what Christ did and we are called to do.

Scholars and scribes long ago recorded the form of the gospel text we have today. They found a specific set of words that Jesus uttered to be required. To that end, each included them in every gospel text (apart from the Gospel of John). These words are: Jesus told his disciples, "You give them something to eat." While such discussions about the authors of the gospels borrowing from one another or out-right copying are well-intentioned, they tend to diminish importance of what these passages have to say to us. These words are a call to action. Disciples of Jesus are to feed the hungry.

FACT: Today, an estimated 821 million people are chronically malnourished.

TRUTH: Jesus calls us to have compassion for one another and to Love our neighbors as we love ourselves. Regardless of where the hungry live; Jesus would consider them our neighbors.

Hunger unchecked is overwhelming. It incapacitates our ability to think about anything else. It saps our energy and leads to increasingly distracted and impulsive decision making. Over time, if left unchecked, chronic hunger becomes malnutrition. Malnutrition involves loss of weight and muscle mass, impacts our immune systems causing an increase in susceptibility to illness, diseases, and poor performance in our tasks. Depending on how quickly our body's resources are diminished, any organ or system in the body can be affected and malfunction. Micronutrients and energy stores are slowly depleted, and the body begins to consume itself to survive. Children who are chronically hungry and malnourished become stunted in both their growth and mental development, contributing to a vicious generational cycle. The struggle is self-sustaining.

Chronic hunger and malnutrition leave people less capable of meeting basic needs, and in turn, less capable of obtaining food. Hunger if unchecked, becomes systemic.

In this study, we will look at the problem of world hunger in light of our Christian faith. In the light of Jesus' command to feed the hungry we will review scripture about grace and compassion (Chapter 1), the scope of the hunger problem (Chapter 2), the barriers of guilt and cynicism that we face as individuals trying to impact hunger issues on a global scale (Chapter 3), how we change our behavior in response to our calling (Chapter 4), and cast a vision for the future (Chapter 5).

In Chapter 1, we will learn that compassion is like a muscle. Built in the image of God, we all have compassion. Like a muscle, some people can build up their strength of compassion much easier than others, but we all can have strong compassion. We are all given the gift of compassion and can ask God for more of it when needed. As a bodybuilder works to build and tone muscle via a disciplined workout routine, we can strengthen our compassion through discipline as well. One of the central ideas we will focus on is how Grace can impact our ability to help end hunger. Together, we can explore what 18th-century minister and founder of the Methodist movement, John Wesley, called the means of grace. We can discover how the means of grace help us to be stronger disciples of Jesus, and as a result, deeply involve God in the challenge of ending hunger.

In Chapter 2, we will see how the issue of hunger is a massive challenge. The number of people who are chronically malnourished is huge! Faced with hungry people, it is easy to be like the disciples and ask Jesus to send the problem away. But in response, Jesus simply says, "You give them something to eat." We all want to make a big impact, don't we? In our small groups and in worship, we talk a lot about how big a difference Jesus made in people's lives. We even have these documented examples of him feeding multitudes! How do we do that? I don't know about you, but I was not born with super abilities to feel compassion

Introduction

for others. I don't have a "pumped up" sense of what justice looks like. My resources are not much greater than anyone else's. Does God expect us to quit school or our day job and devote our every waking moment to the task of 'you give them something to eat'? Really? Is it all on our shoulders? Maybe we're biting off more than an individual can chew. Considering these questions, we can look deeper into the perception of just how big this hunger problem is and how big God is in comparison.

In Chapter 3, we will face the forces that oppose our response to the problem of world hunger. If compassion is the grease that lubricates our gears to seek justice on behalf of those who hunger, then guilt is a handful of sand tossed into the mechanism. Have you ever felt shame because you don't have the burden of wondering where your next meal will come from, or because your last meal was the equivalent of an impoverished person's monthly wages? The simple solution to eliminating the guilt is just to live poor, right? Nope. Have you ever heard someone say something like, "When has becoming poor yourself ever helped anyone who is already poor?" That kind of thought process is a product of a cynical worldview and places you at the center of the problem and not the people who are chronically malnourished.

If compassion is the grease that lubricates our gears to see justice, then cynicism is a foreign object flung into the machine that stops all the works from turning. Cynicism stops all progress and is purely an attitude that can be prevented. For those who are already cynical about ending world hunger, by the time we get to this chapter, we will seek to use Holy Scripture to ease your mind.

In Chapter 4, I hope you've become excited about joining me in Fasting, Prayer, and Giving to end hunger. I also hope that you've identified the secret sauce to how discipleship plays into these actions and how the universal church, as the body of Christ, can lead the efforts to end hunger. If not, this chapter might help you along as we look at behavior change and how to apply what we've learned.

In the final chapter, we look at the vision cast (spoilers!) of a world without hunger because Christians choose to tap into the means of grace and fulfill their theological task.

The Wesley Quadrilateral

On occasion, you'll see a reference to the Wesley Quadrilateral. This concept is really borrowing ideas from one of the founders of the Methodist Movement, John Wesley, on how to source information to arrive at theological conclusions. It became a methodology and therefore defined the process by which early Methodists (see the root word Method in both Methodist and Methodology?) could be "methodical" in working out theological questions. This process relies on four pillars of guidance: Scripture, Tradition, Experience, and Reason.

Scripture – the Bible. The best and only words of God we have captured in a tangible fixed form.

Tradition – People have been following the teachings of the Bible for a long time. We must have something to show for over two thousand years of Christianity. We do: it's called tradition.

Experience – When we live through faith, which we define the belief in things unseen, the proof is often elusive, but the experience is personal and real.

Reason – We are created in God's image. Our ability to combine facts and thoughts into functional and complex statements is proof of this. We have a God-given ability to reason.

Introduction

I've learned that if each of the four areas of the quadrilateral can be applied logically and share at least a portion of the authority in how my beliefs are shaped, I'm usually on the right path. Use it as you see fit. A word of caution: not all four sources of the Wesleyan quadrilateral must have equal importance in defining our beliefs. Scripture is the primary lens through which all the other sources are viewed. There are many great resources on the Wesleyan Quadrilateral. I encourage you to seek them out.

In this study, the most flexible and versatile piece of each lesson I call "quadrilateralize," which is a combination of words that I find amusing. I envision the term to describe a measuring stick or litmus test by which I can discern if my thoughts and feelings are consistent with the guidance of the Holy Spirit. It is intended as a tool for you to apply the same test when putting your Christian beliefs into practice. I have taken the four areas of the Wesleyan Quadrilateral and tried to ask questions of each to spur either discussion or thought on how the lesson passes the test of being solid guidance for spritiual formation.

GOALS TO BE ACHIEVED BY THIS STUDY

This study is a companion to go along with a set of practices that are focused around a change event; ending hunger. Albeit, this is just a bunch of words on paper that should spark dialogue, but I hope that it becomes more. I hope you find reasons to change how you live. I believe deeply involving God in our daily lives can position our talents and resources to make a significant impact in our lifetime. I hope you join us at FastPrayGive.org and be a part of the movement to end hunger. I hope you take up fasting as a spiritual practice. I hope you lean deeper into sacrificing for others, not only in a financial gift, but also with a gift of your time. I hope because of this study you spend more time in prayer and in service to others. Most of all, I hope you put into action all the means of grace we will talk about in this study and in-turn find opportunities to be in communion with those who are the most vulnerable, even if it is only in spirit.

Those are some lofty actions to take on as goals. I want to throw one more goal out. My final hope is that you offer this same call to others, that as you grow along the path of discipleship, you might invite others to join you.

Chapter 1:

That's a lot of Grace

Luke 15:11-32 | Matthew 20:1-16 | Luke 10:25-37
What does grace look like?

James 4:6 | 1 Peter 4:10 | Ephesians 2:8-9
How do we interact with grace?

It is the grace of God that helps those who do everything that lies within their power to achieve that which is beyond their power.
– ABRAHAM JOSHUA HESCHEL

By "means of grace" I understand outward signs, words, or actions, ordained of God, and appointed for this end, to be the ordinary channels whereby He might convey to men, preventing, justifying, or sanctifying grace. -JOHN WESLEY (Sermon 16)

The Description and Definition of Grace

I know a guy who makes furniture and art out of pallet wood. This often-discarded lumber is redeemed and put to good use. I asked him to make a piece of wall art for me to display against the back wall of my house. I wanted it to be a focal point in my back yard. I have a nice shady spot on the back wall of my house by my hanging porch swing.

He asked me via a text message what I wanted it to look like, and I told him I wanted a word. I told him I wanted it to be five letters that spell GRACE. He followed up with a question, "how big?" I told him the dimensions which were at least three feet tall for each letter. His response was, "Wow!! That's a lot of grace!!!", and it made me think. Yea! There is a reason I want it that big, not just to fill the wall space, but because I feel like grace has been the biggest influence in my life since I came to understand it (at least since I started to believe that I understand it**). Ask yourself this question: Can I explain what grace is to someone who doesn't know anything about it?** Its description, let alone what it does or how it works, is not easy to explain in layman's terms.

In this chapter we'll explore what grace is and what does grace have to do with ending hunger? Simply put, God is in the business of grace. In our relationship with God, grace is possibly the most defining feature. We will also look at how I came to understand grace and explain it. My methods, reasons, and explanations might be very different from yours. For a long time, I was apprehensive about trying to put these things into words, because it might not make sense to someone else. Finally, we'll explore the means of grace and how we build the practices that develop our relationship with God and further puts us to use in ending hunger. The way in which we ask for help and receive it is nuanced, and that is why we must first dig deeper to understand and be able to explain grace to one another.

What is grace to the hungry?

Grace is as impactful as it is important. It's a topic that is as deep as the oceans' trenches to as tall as the farthest star we can see in the night sky. I recognize that Grace has dimension and depth, which stretches human understanding as a concept. The complexity and difficulty in understanding the nuances in how different people understand, interact, and perceive Grace is great. Sometimes I don't know where to start. For this, let's start by using our imagination.

Visualize yourself as someone who has no idea where their next meal is coming from. Imagine a scenario in which you have no employment and no assets of value. If you will, add on top of that either an inability to work or situation where if you did work, your labor earned too little to be meaningful or your earnings were stolen by criminals, or taken from you by an oppressive regime or government. Conceptualize a reality where all paths lead to continued poverty and inescapable misfortune. What would be your mental state if you survived this by digging through the trash or putting your entire family to work (children included) so that you could languish at the edge of starvation, racked with anxiety over food?

I tried to paint a picture with words of real-world situations that would lead to hopelessness. A situation which is so dire, one can't comprehend how to get out and from which hope cannot thrive, let alone exist. Hope is one of the single greatest forms of nourishment that is not physical. Hope has lifted people from poverty, helped lead revolutions, and end wars. Hope is not only an expectation of a positive outcome but a mantra that we cherish, and when it is gone, we lament. How do we put hope back into the life of someone who is without hope? How do we replenish it for the person in the visualization exercise we just completed?

I used to think food gives hope to the malnourished. I was mostly wrong. **Grace gives hope to the hopeless.** If you can't wrangle yourself out of poverty, someone has to help you out. If you remain in poverty, or on the edge of poverty, and you are not starving, it is because someone gave you food. Someone acted with grace and gave a gift. There was a need for compassion, and the need was filled. Food is merely one vehicle that delivers all kinds of compassion to the hurting or provides justice to the oppressed. Food to the malnourished **is** grace. Grace exists in actions, whether tangible, physical, logical, or ethereal. You can personally feed someone, you can package meals, you can design systems and methods to meet needs, or you can deliver impactful advocacy on behalf of someone who needs food. Grace exists in actions we might do, like feeding the hungry but is not solely defined by the action.

Take a moment and think about or talk about, if you are in a group, how you would explain what grace is to someone who is unfamiliar with the concept. How do you define grace?

Grace in the larger context

So here is how I explain it: Grace is a gift that God gives that we may or may not know we want. It can, at times, be alternatively described as salvation, blessings, or good favor. Whether we have received grace or not, we can share it. Grace is unearned; it is free; it is undeserved. For example, God took human form in Jesus Christ and died to take on the debt of our sins. God gave us salvation, and that is an example of the **gift** of God's Grace. I know with the mention of 'debt' and 'gift' it sounds kind of like a donation or a financial transaction, but stick with me, because grace does not have an assigned earthly value. Grace is like an interaction between our creator and us. It also can exist as an interaction between humans. It's a big intangible thing with sometimes tangible results. I've just thrown a bunch of concepts around, but I've not clearly defined grace the way you might find it in a dictionary.

It's a big concept to wrap a definition around. We should break it into parts. For centuries scholars have looked at different parts of how grace is central to our relationship with God. In the Wesleyan tradition, we have three big terms; there is *prevenient grace,* which is given by God when we don't even know we need it. It's a gift we didn't expect to receive. I like to think of prevenient grace as the mysterious desire to be closer to God and the capability to understand and have faith. Without the embedded instinct to seek a creator, where would we be? That yearning for God is the initial gift of grace. God knows, loves, and cares for us deeply, even if we've not yet become aware of the existence of God. *Justifying grace* brings us into alignment with God. Salvation is provided as part of the deal. It is activated specifically with the turning point in which we are given the strength to adjust course in our lives and focus on God. We are enabled to access this gift by God's action through Jesus Christ. We are assured of salvation through the presence of the Holy Spirit. All we must do is respond faithfully. There is also *sanctifying grace,* which is the gift that keeps on giving. It is the grace that allows us to get better at being followers of Jesus. In turn, we get better at doing God's work. Sanctification literally means "set apart for a particular purpose and to make sacred." Many people treat salvation as the end of the faith journey. The work must continue beyond the moment of being "saved." We will make mistakes and sin, but this grace motivates us to grow, mature, and strive to live as Christ did. That is how we become 'set apart.' Wesleyans often like to repeat how John Wesley once described grace as a house. Prevenient grace is the front porch, which is sheltered and inviting, justifying grace is the front door by which we enter, and sanctifying grace is the inside of the house which we can reside and grow. Sometimes I get a bit overwhelmed and think, "Wow!! That's a lot of grace!!!"

Means of Grace

John Wesley, the founder of the Methodist Movement, threw out this term that has stuck around called, Means of Grace. "Means" is not a term we use very much. The "means to an end" is about the only common phrase in my vernacular outside of means of grace. The means is really the way you go about something. Means is the steps toward completion, or tasks at hand to get the job done. It's a throw-back phrase from days gone by, but I'm not willing to toss it aside. In fact, I think it perks up the ear and requires someone to ponder the meaning.

Wesley didn't write down his beliefs and say, "this is what the Methodist church will believe." Wesley documented **why** we do **what** we do as Christians and **how** we should go about doing it. The means of grace are the actions we do, so that God can work through us and inside us. They strengthen our faith (relationship) and do so by outward (although sometimes privately) affirmation of our faith. These actions strengthen and grow our faith; our faith demands we love our God and our neighbor and therefore generate grace on behalf of God. To create more Grace, Wesley simply documented the method by which he arrived at. He started with scripture, looked at faith traditions, examined his experiences, and reasoned out the best possible methodology. The preaching that followed bore out why we work to bring about more grace and how we go about the task. You can read more about how, as Methodists, we discern our beliefs. Insight into how early Methodists (and current Methodists) beliefs are shaped, formed, and informed by reading about the Wesleyan Quadrilateral. More on the quadrilateral is found in the introduction.

Sanctification relies on Means of Grace, which Wesley preached at length about. Just like with grace, we have some sub-sections to consider. **Works of Piety,** which includes prayer, reading scripture, fasting, taking part in communion, Christian fellowship, and healthy living. After all, piety means being reverent or religious. These works of piety are those that if you performed them regularly, someone might consider you spirit-filled or religious. **Works of Mercy** work the same way; they are things you could do that might get you labeled as merciful. This is stuff like doing good in general, like visiting the sick and imprisoned, visiting with those who mourn, feeding the hungry, helping the poor, and giving generously.

To make sure I clarify, performing these means of grace listed above don't earn salvation, God already gives that grace to us as a gift (prevenient grace), and we understand and accept it (justifying grace). These are the things we do to serve God better and strengthen our relationship (sanctifying grace). They are the keys to the car, the passcode to our phones, the secret handshake at the club. Fun Fact: FastPrayGive.org uses means of grace to deeply involve God in humanity's fight to end chronic malnutrition and hunger.

Reflection Questions

Explain In your own words (based on life experience) what is Grace?

What specifically has God's grace done for you?

What does Grace do for us (as a people)?

How do the Means of Grace lead to sanctification?

What role can sanctification place in ending world hunger?

Quadrilateralize

Scripture – Where is grace described or defined in scripture? How does the scripture shape your belief about God and grace?

Tradition – What part of our history as Christians has solidified grace as an essential part of our relationship with God?

Experience – Where has grace been evident in your life? Do you have a "once blind, but now I see" moment?

Reason – What new thoughts come to mind after reading about, reflecting on, and considering God's grace?

Chapter 2:

The Perception of Hunger

Isaiah 61:1 | Mark 10:23-27

The act of drawing sharpens the perceptions of the draftsman
-JOHN RUSKIN

WE WANT TO SHARE THE grace of God by helping our neighbor in need. What a BIG job. To understand how badly help is needed in some parts of the world, I think about cookies. In some parts of the world, the only meal a child might get each day is cookies. Sounds great, right? Well. No. In places hit by poverty, food essentials like meat, rice, or vegetables are too expensive, and the only choice might be an unwelcome alternative. In places like Haiti, dirt is hauled to the market, and there are people who purchase it. They purchase it for a price that you and I would consider to be WAY too high for dirt. They add salt and some shortening (fat) to the dirt to form a mud cookie which is left out in the sun to bake. Children are fed these cookies. Adults eat them, but rarely in public, because they are embarrassed.

This practice has a name. ***Geophagy****: the practice of eating dirt, clay, or chalk.*

When you live on less than $2 a week, the mud cookie might be all you can afford. Some people make mud cookies to sell. They form the basis of an economy for some folks, but for most they fill a need. The people who buy, sell, and consume mud cookies are not proud of it. As I said, many are embarrassed by it. The children do not know any different. The mud cookie stops hunger pains. I've not eaten one,

The Perception of Hunger

but first-hand accounts I've read say when they touch your mouth, they instantly absorb all the moisture from your pallet. This leaves you with a dry mouth and temporarily appeased hunger pangs. The bitter taste remains for hours. It is gut-wrenching (figuratively) to hear that even this is preferable to the pain of a truly empty stomach.

This is just one of many examples of the type of intolerable suffering that exists in our world. I think all you must do is **hear** about mud cookies, and you know there is a problem worth solving. I believe the problem is two-fold:

First, there are 821 million chronically malnourished people in the world.

Second, there is a lack of hope that the first problem can be resolved.

Obviously, the hungry person can struggle with seeing a way out of a desperate situation. What a struggle it must be to even dream of a life where food is readily available. To those of us living outside and far away from these conditions, we can empathize on how utterly depressing this must be. Even from afar we can see how difficult this situation is to overcome. To be clear, I think we (the affluent and well-nourished) must find hope as well as those in need to bring about an end to hunger — more on hope in a bit.

Let's talk about the problem

My rudimentary problem-solving skills tell me. First, we must understand the problem. Then, we can seek the root cause, and begin to formulate a solution. We might even postulate a theory (for my scientist friends) somewhere in the process.

Hunger isn't just this thing that is out there to be resolved. I believe that no one is naive enough to believe that it is a problem that is "fixed" by flipping a non-governmental, International, Humanitarian Aid switch. Hunger is a complex deal with complex causes. There is no bad guy with henchmen that creates the world's hunger problem. I think we're all to blame. I caused hunger; you are creating hunger; we all will continue to create hunger. Please don't be upset because I'm spreading the blame around. I'll walk you through my thought process on how I got here.

Everyone on the earth is part of our family. If you follow the pastoral tale of creation and walk forward, we all end up with Adam and Eve as our ancestors. Setting aside any debate about how we got to where we are today, you must agree that our differences are only in how the DNA building blocks of our bodies are arranged. God created the heavens and the earth, created humans, and gave us the ability to understand and comprehend the science we have before us today. The form of each person on this planet is not vastly different. All of us stand upright; we have symmetrical bodies with arms, legs, ears, nose, and eyes. Where we become distinct is a varied arrangement and expression of the same building blocks that make up our consistent form. Every single one of us is nothing but a different combination of the same ingredients. Don't believe me? Get lost in the education section of genetic ancestry-testing websites. They are getting pretty good at identifying people who are 5th cousins who live on different continents via DNA testing alone. We're **all** so similar, scientists classify us all as Homo Sapiens. People living in different quadrant of our planet, though they may talk with a different accent which sounds funny to your ears, are **all** still Homo Sapiens. The person living atop a mountain in Chile is no different fundamentally than the person living high in the Swiss Alps. Last time I checked, ALL only means one thing…everyone, with no exceptions. We're all family.

Back to the cause of the problem: Hunger exists because we refuse to live in a communal way with our human family. Every one of us in one way or another have rejected other Homo Sapiens as our family members. You may think you've not rejected anyone but hear me out. The most persistent causes of hunger are the direct result of poverty.

The Perception of Hunger

Poverty can be caused by a lack of resources, environmental changes, or by oppression. All of which can be a direct result of human interaction. Many people cite climate change as an example of increasing human-related influence. All these human-impacted conditions are at least indirectly caused by greed. Greed is a result of an inherent basal level of selfishness. You may have heard the buzzword term, "fear of scarcity," as the underlying description of the selfish emotional state. What is selfishness? It is caring about yourself more than **other people**, right? **Other people** make up the world, which is inhabited by your human family. I'm not saying God expects you to invite every other person on the planet to your family reunion this summer. However, I want you to expand your theological definition of family for the sake of grasping the root cause of the problem.

I'm not saying you individually have oppressed someone or stolen their power, but have you actively done anything to prevent the theft? We all participate in a society that encourages, rewards, and revels in power. Even though you are only one person in billions that reside on our planet, one could say we're all responsible for this scourge. Everyone is fractional if not infinitesimally complicit. Let me be clear; I don't expect you to overthrow a brutal dictator or quit your job to change hearts and minds about greed. God does not expect us to take on that task alone. Hunger is a huge problem with a set of root causes so large they cannot be counted. Thinking about it make me feel the size of an ant looking at the empire state building. I think size and scale is an important thing to consider here. More on that later.

Now that we know where the cause begins, how do we change our path as Christians to make a difference? How does our path impact the world at large? These are questions that smart and compassionate people have been trying to answer for a long time. Plans have been put into action, and few have resulted in success. What little progress that has been made pales in comparison to the ridiculous-sized problem that still exists. Many people tried, and many people failed because they perceived the ridiculous-sized problem as easy or simple to solve. Conversely, they may have seen their significant contribution as insignificant and become disappointed because of the immense forces at work.

LET'S TALK ABOUT SIZE

> GENESIS 15:5-6 (GOD'S COVENANT WITH ABRAM)
> *HE BROUGHT HIM OUTSIDE AND SAID, "LOOK TOWARD HEAVEN AND COUNT THE STARS, IF YOU ARE ABLE TO COUNT THEM." THEN HE SAID TO HIM, "SO SHALL YOUR DESCENDANTS BE." AND HE BELIEVED THE LORD; AND THE LORD RECKONED IT TO HIM AS RIGHTEOUSNESS.*

Though God created us in his image, we have a tough time understanding the measurements required. If you're into science, you might enjoy a book called *A Short History of Nearly Everything* by Bill Bryson. It neatly fills the void of both an anecdotal history of science and the infamous or little-known figures that created and discovered what we know today. In addition, the author distills and summarizes the reasons why it is so very important to us as a society. I think Bryson helped me see the scope by which our God works. Did you know you and I are huge compared to things measured at the sub-microscopic level? There are things so small that we can't see them with a microscope. Bryson writes, "A Proton is an infinitesimal part of an atom, which is itself, of course, an insubstantial thing. Protons are so small that a little dib of ink like the dot on this *i* can hold something in the region of 500,000,000,000 of them, rather more than the number of seconds contained in half a million years." People on the internet who claim to know about these things say there are nearly 7,000,000,000,000,000,000,000,000,000 protons in a human body.

The Perception of Hunger

(Pronounced: Seven Octillion or seven billion billion, or seven thousand trillion-trillion)

At the same time, wrap your head around the vastness of God's creation: At the time of its writing, Bryon's book boast, "...there are perhaps 140 billion galaxies in the visible universe." A cursory internet search today will take you to a Wikipedia article stating a current estimate is between 200 billion and 10 trillion galaxies. Maybe the difference is because Bryson's book was written before the last upgrade to the Hubble Space telescope which continues to expand our measurements of what we cannot see above our heads in the night sky. If you dig around NASA's website, you'll find they estimate there are maybe 100 to 200 billion stars in our Milky Way galaxy. If our galaxy is any indication of how many stars are in the sky, we're looking up at a conservative estimate of two sextillion stars. Do you have trouble visualizing that? In numbers that's 2,000,000,000,000,000,000,000. (which is 200 billion galaxies with 100 billion stars each – the more conservative figures I can find).

Genesis 13:16
I WILL MAKE YOUR OFFSPRING LIKE THE DUST OF THE EARTH; SO THAT IF ONE CAN COUNT THE DUST OF THE EARTH, YOUR OFFSPRING ALSO CAN BE COUNTED.

These examples of scripture and our current understanding are not meant to dissuade you from attempting to grasp the complexity of God. I'm also not trying to start a debate on science and if someone could really count the specks of dust on the earth. I'm trying to point out that there are possibly things smaller than we understand and a vastness that is so large we cannot understand it. Why don't we do like Abram (Genesis 15:5-6) and have faith that God has a firm grip on the issue and stop trying to calculate the exact approach to a resolution? Trying to perceive, understand, and contemplate all the issues causing systemic hunger in human terms with numbers, calculus, or even geometry is fruitless.

FastPrayGive

The way God measures hunger is through hope or hopelessness.

Let's talk about Hope

Isaiah 61:1
The Spirit of the Sovereign LORD is on me, because the LORD has anointed me to proclaim good news to the poor. He has sent me to bind up the brokenhearted, to proclaim freedom for the captives and release from darkness for the prisoners.

The solution for ending hunger is the destruction of hopelessness. That is done when we restore the hope of our human family. We become the vehicle of God answering a prayer to end hunger. We restore the faith of others by ourselves being faithful. When we believe that – it is GAME OVER for hunger.

Now, how do we gather and distribute hope? Just like grace, in chapter 1, we are talking about something that is intangible with tangible results. More specifically, I point you back to the means of grace and the works of Mercy to restore hope. Use the means of grace to find hope, restore hope to others, and as a byproduct end hunger.

"But you can't eat hope!" is the exclamation someone will make. When we pray for God to put us to use in the movement to end hunger, and when we earn, save, and give generously, we can share food with others. When we focus on the health and wellbeing of our neighbors first, we restore hope. The United Nations Food and Agriculture Organization (FAO) reports that we grow enough food for 10 Billion people, and yet there are only about 8 Billion people on earth. Yet 1 in 9 people are chronically malnourished and 20,000 people each day will die from hunger related causes. Neither food or hope is a production problem; it is a passion problem.

Jesus stood up in the synagogue and read the passage from Isaiah above. Jesus was reading a passage about God's grace being shared as good news, and that, in sharing the good news, we would bring hope (bind up the brokenhearted). Then he told everyone in attendance that, "Today this scripture is fulfilled in your hearing." Jesus is telling everyone that hope is coming. Let's use the means of grace to bring hope to the hungry.

Reflection Questions

How do we change our perception to see hunger as God sees hunger?

How might grace help us to understand hope/hopelessness better?

Quadrilateralize

Scripture – Are there other places in scripture where Jesus tries to change his disciple's perception of God's capabilities?

Tradition – What part of our history as Christian disciples affirms our belief that with God's help, we can tackle the biggest of problems?

Experience – When have you entrusted a problem to God that was just "too big" to be resolved alone? What was the outcome?

Reason – Does the application of God's scale of measurement cause us to adjust our perception of hunger, sin, and hopelessness?

FastPrayGive

Chapter 3:

Defeating Guilt and Cynicism

Zechariah 3:9-10 | Luke 4:18-19 | Mark 10:27

ZECHARIAH 3:9-10
FOR ON THE STONE THAT I HAVE SET BEFORE JOSHUA, ON A SINGLE STONE WITH SEVEN FACETS, I WILL ENGRAVE ITS INSCRIPTION, SAYS THE LORD OF HOSTS, AND I WILL REMOVE THE GUILT OF THIS LAND IN A SINGLE DAY. ON THAT DAY, SAYS THE LORD OF HOSTS, YOU SHALL INVITE EACH OTHER TO COME UNDER YOUR VINE AND FIG TREE.

IT IS MY HOPE THAT you see the multi-faceted problem of global malnutrition or "hunger" in a new light. Possibly your vision is enhanced with a wider scope, but a narrower focus. You can see the problem of nearly a billion malnourished souls as God-sized and yet that shouldn't scare us. However, there are pitfalls to avoid, snares and traps to circumnavigate, and lo and behold, the devil is hiding in the weeds. I know you're getting ready to put the means of grace to use and join the movement to end hunger, but I want to share some caution about two of the most difficult hurdles you might have to overcome. In this chapter, we'll attempt to address two of the elephants in the room. First, we'll look at how Guilt and Cynicism are born, grow, and are fed. At the same time, we'll discuss a path to overcome them for the sake of working to end hunger.

Defeating Guilt and Cynicism

GUILT AND SHAME

I have experienced a good bit of shame about the disparities that exist between countries that have a lot of resources and those that don't. It took me a while to label it. I was not sure why I felt that way or what to call it, but after careful reflection and prayer, here is where I stand:

On one occasion, I was sent to Las Vegas for a work conference, and I was invited each night by partners of my employer to eat at some of the most popular and elegant restaurants in town. Each night I enjoyed imported delicacies prepared by world-class chefs in restaurants owned by celebrity chefs and celebrities alike. One night a small number of us were taken to a sushi restaurant where we didn't even order food. The chef just prepared dishes and waiters delivered food as a "meal experience." It was an experience to remember, but after I returned to my hotel room, I felt uneasy about it. It was not the raw fish as I love sushi. I was not sure why I was bothered. I was struggling to identify my feelings. Has that ever happened to you? Here is what I figured out.

At the end of our opulent meal, I happened to see the bill with a **four-digit price** slide across the table to our host. I felt a little funny at the time, but later that night, I had a rather large feeling of guilt and regret. The portion of the meal I had eaten could have fed over five hundred people through an international feeding program. I felt remorse. I asked God for forgiveness.

At first, I tried to wipe off the guilt and in-turn masked it as shame. What is the difference? You feel guilty when you do something bad, but shame is when you bury it and start to feel as though you are a bad person. Feeling guilty and resolving to do something about it is transformative. Feeling shame is the result of letting your shortcoming define you internally if not outwardly. Both shame and guilt are natural human emotions we should all have. The challenge is recognizing them and building perspective to grow as individuals. The best result is using them to adjust our lives to be healthy and not live in a cycle of distress and depression.

I didn't ask for that super-expensive meal in Vegas. I don't eat this way all the time. I do make donations to international aid organizations. I'm a hunger warrior…I'm not a bad guy. Why should I feel bad? I felt a twinge of anger. And then I slipped back into guilt…what about advocacy? I didn't speak up on behalf of the hungry. I beat myself up emotionally, "I sat there quietly! I treated the malnourished unjustly. I am the worst and should be ashamed". I didn't bring the issue to everyone's attention at the table that we were treating ourselves so much better than we treat our human neighbors. After all, Jesus commanded that we love our neighbors as we love ourselves.

After further thought, I realized I might NEVER be able to say those types of things out loud, because it could have major repercussions like losing my job. I can't stand up and throw ideas like that in my co-workers' and host's face. Nobody likes to do business with the people who make you feel bad. How could I be so very rude? How could I be ungrateful for the gesture made by my employer's partner? At different times and in different places over the next few weeks, the battle raged on in my head. You may think that I was spiraling out of control over something I had little control over. That fact didn't matter. I kept thinking that I was complicit in the ongoing hunger of my human family. There are people eating mud cookies, for goodness sake! Am I overly sensitive? Why am I wallowing in shame? Have I gone off the deep end? How did I get stuck in this position?

I pondered potential courses of action. Could I make a change and take a stand on such excesses at all costs to myself? Could I avoid work trips and fain illness to skip having these kinds of meals out with our vendors? Should I just keep doing what I was doing and beg God for forgiveness because of my inaction?

Defeating Guilt and Cynicism

Ultimately, taking a stand publicly was not an action I felt like would yield reasonable results, and seemed more likely to offend my colleagues. Avoiding a few work meals by claiming I had a headache or making an excuse to go back to my hotel room could only work for so long. Asking God to forgive my flagrant disregard for other people's need *without* making a change seemed wrong. I felt I could not ask for forgiveness for what I ate, what it cost, or why I didn't speak up. Why? Because my begging for forgiveness was only seeking to end my temporary feeling of guilt and my sliding into a deep pit of shame. I was stumped.

I did not know how to change my behavior (repent). Taking clear action could have caused a lot of trouble for me. My job paid my salary and afforded me the ability to make donations to and work with humanitarian aid organizations. My work compensation helped me to tithe so that the church could do great works in my community and around the world as well as make a new generation of disciples. John Wesley is famously quoted for saying: "Earn all you can, save all you can, give all you can."

So, I prayed for God to change my motivation from absolving myself of guilt or getting me out of the moral dilemma. Instead, I asked God to help me listen and asked, "What do you want me to do, Lord?" I wanted to hear how God wanted to put me to use to end hunger. Immediately, I wondered, "Why don't I have this kind of discussion with God more often?" I need to be in more frequent communication with God about where my motivation comes from and where it resides in relation to my guilt for the things I did and the shame for the things I didn't do (that I should do). During this time of prayer and earnestly listening, God and I had a very frank chat, and it largely revolved around redirecting my motivation from being guilty to me asking to really be "put to doing" something about ending hunger

I committed to a new approach. My fight against hunger would not be MINE, but it would be also God's. It would be ours. I would daily ask God for direction and worry less about what judgment was to come.

What do you know? God answers prayers. God has since placed lots of opportunities in front of me to work on behalf of the suffering. By better living into the calling that God had placed on me, I am able to put aside guilt and focus on the task of helping in God's work. All I had to do was ask.

Coincidentally, I've not been invited to a similarly swanky meal since. Especially a meal, which I would categorize it as wholly and totally inappropriate in the face of those who hunger. I am still not sure what words I might use to politely decline a request to eat at such a super-expensive restaurant. I know I would make it solely about my choice to not participate and not an attempt to heap guilt on someone else over their choices. If pressed, I might share my reasoning that God has given Christians a calling to love their neighbor including the hungry, and part of my commitment to God is self-denial (fasting) of meals that broaden the massive inequality between me and those who are chronically malnourished.

Caution: You should never feel guilty because you went to a nice restaurant. Use your instincts on the difference between 'nice' and 'obscene' and avoid the latter. Neither should you feel guilty when you head to the grocery for prime ingredients for a celebration or a special occasion. Instead of feeling guilty or shame, feel empowered to ask God to bless your food so that you might be strong enough to fight the hunger of those who are in need, to hear God's calling, and to seek out ways to help our neighbors. Also, the problem is not ours to face alone. In the same way that God calls to each one of us individually to help solve hunger, he also calls the entire church. Each one of us needs to be prepared to carry our share of the burden the way an individual muscle cell lends its strength to the biceps or triceps so that our arm can swing a hammer to crush hunger.

Defeating Guilt and Cynicism

Cynicism

Mark 14:7
For you always have the poor with you, and you can show kindness to them whenever you wish; but you will not always have me.

In the next chapter, we'll talk more about behavior change. Ultimately, becoming disciples of Christ who add the practices of the means of grace into our lives requires a behavior change. Like guilt, one of the major hurdles in ending hunger and changing our behavior to effect change is cynicism. It's easy to be skeptical or negative about stuff today. Of 558 emotion words in the English language, 62% are negative. There is the old saying, "The Yupik languages of the Inuit people have over 100 words for snow." With over 300 different negative emotion-related words at our disposal, negativity must be our society's snow.

I struggle a lot of days to deal with the pressure that there are MILLIONS of people who need our help. Add to it the knowledge that the behavioral change necessary to help those in need it is not easy. There is a significant escape hatch that is always nearby. I call it the "can't" escape hatch. **We can't do it. They can't do it. It can't be done.** I feel like around every corner is an opportunity to make an excuse and pull the fire alarm and make an orderly exit on any effort to bring hunger to an end. Some days I bring it on myself but can persevere and stay strong…until I encounter someone else, who reinforces my doubts. The one excuse I get slapped with on occasion is that my efforts are admirable but wasted because even Jesus said, "the poor will always be with you…" It honestly stings.

There is this thing called "proof-texting." It's the idea that you can pick up a biblical concordance (a book that helps you find bible verses based on a word or idea) or search the internet and find scripture that meets your needs even if it's truncated or taken out of context. For example, check out the scripture from Zechariah at the beginning of this chapter. It has words like facet and guilt and seems to match up with the general flavor of this study. It even ends with verse 10 talking about everyone having their own vine and fig tree; translation: abundant food. It's even better than anything I hoped to find! The scripture seems to end with the reader being foretold about a time where we will be invited to sit (probably leisurely in the shade) under the vine and fig tree. Vines grow fruit like grapes…which we eat or make a beverage. (sounds like a picnic to me and the end to hunger) The honest truth is that story from Zachariah has **little** to do with hunger or guilt related to it.

George Washington quoted this or the many other scriptural references to 'vine and fig tree' in his letters. Washington often used it to describe a well-earned reward, or a place of rest, safety, and security. I really think it's scripture about Christ's return and the impact it will have on all people. It's a prophecy. At the end of the prophecy, it says that we will all share in God's grace, and we'll invite others to share it as well. It stands by itself without trying to apply it to our cause at hand, and it remains powerful. Nothing, however, stopped me from searching for the word Guilt in a concordance and trying to apply it to my purpose.

With that in mind, let's look at one of the greatest cynical proof text examples in history. I think of using this scripture of "the poor will always be with you" as a way to get out of helping our neighbors. This has to be in the *cynical idea hall-of-fame* (not a thing…yet, maybe I should trademark it!) First, you should read all of it in context. **Matthew 26:6-13** Secondly, the statement is not a prophecy as nay-sayers would have you believe, but it is a declaratory statement. Jesus is stating a fact. Even if there is no one who starves to death or is hungry on a consistent basis, poverty will not cease to exist. Poverty can be due to lack of resources, education, opportunity, safety, spirit, time…you name it. People can survive poverty, but that does not mean we consider it acceptable to exist. Third, Jesus is making this statement to his disciples, people who have already left behind their possessions to follow him around the countryside, and help…you guessed it… the poor, on a daily basis. Fourth, in this chapter, Jesus is facing the prospect of His imminent crucifixion. He is grieving in advance, and the gift of the woman's expensive oil is a great comfort to him as he prepares for his trial of suffering and death. Finally, I've even had people tell me Jesus is telling his followers that He (Jesus) is more important than poor people. To them, I would respond that Jesus makes it clear throughout the gospels that **the most important thing to Him is that we follow His lead by loving God and our neighbor,** and that the way we show this is by loving "the least of these my brethren." Let's look at the verse again, with context, this time from Matthew.

MATTHEW 26:6-13
WHILE JESUS WAS IN BETHANY IN THE HOME OF SIMON THE LEPER, A WOMAN CAME TO HIM WITH AN ALABASTER JAR OF VERY EXPENSIVE PERFUME, WHICH SHE POURED ON HIS HEAD AS HE WAS RECLINING AT THE TABLE.
WHEN THE DISCIPLES SAW THIS, THEY WERE INDIGNANT. "WHY THIS WASTE?" THEY ASKED. "THIS PERFUME COULD HAVE BEEN SOLD AT A HIGH PRICE AND THE MONEY GIVEN TO THE POOR."
AWARE OF THIS, JESUS SAID TO THEM, "WHY ARE YOU BOTHERING THIS WOMAN? SHE HAS DONE A BEAUTIFUL THING TO ME. THE POOR YOU WILL ALWAYS HAVE WITH YOU,[4] BUT YOU WILL NOT ALWAYS HAVE ME WHEN SHE POURED THIS PERFUME ON MY BODY, SHE DID IT TO PREPARE ME FOR BURIAL. TRULY I TELL YOU, WHEREVER THIS GOSPEL IS PREACHED THROUGHOUT THE WORLD, WHAT SHE HAS DONE WILL ALSO BE TOLD, IN MEMORY OF HER."

The truth is that this scripture, in context, isn't about poverty and the existence of it. Rather it's about the **brief** and **human** existence of God (as Jesus) who came for a limited time to show us a path to salvation. Jesus was comforting his friends and is also comforted by the woman's generous gift. It was good timing because Jesus' sacrifice was only a few days away, and with it would come to the completion of his primary mission in service to God the Father. Without Christ's suffering, death, and resurrection, there would be no hope for a lasting relationship with God. Failed covenant after failed covenant had only resulted in humanity's broken relationship with God until Jesus' arrival to set things right. Our brokenness made it impossible for humans to even be in alignment with God. Without first repairing our broken relationship with God, there is no way we could successfully tackle God-sized problems like poverty, feeding the hungry, bringing freedom for the oppressed, or giving sight to the blind.

> LUKE 4:18-19
>
> *THE SPIRIT OF THE LORD IS ON ME, BECAUSE HE HAS ANOINTED ME TO PROCLAIM GOOD NEWS TO THE POOR. HE HAS SENT ME TO PROCLAIM FREEDOM FOR THE PRISONERS AND RECOVERY OF SIGHT FOR THE BLIND, TO SET THE OPPRESSED FREE, TO PROCLAIM THE YEAR OF THE LORD'S FAVOR.*

Through exegesis (an uncommon word which means a critical interpretation or explanation of the text), we can find that a cynical, out of context interpretation of this scripture is ignorant of the hope that is the solution to the problem. In Christ's sacrifice, our relationship with God has been repaired. In God's kingdom, even the poor (who will always be with us) are fed. We, who have been redeemed by Christ to participate in God's work, can become coworkers in bridging the gap between God's kingdom and our present circumstances.

I think God knows the difference between poverty and chronic hunger, and if, in our cynicism, we are still having a hard time, consider the tenth chapter of Mark, which is a passage about salvation and its relationship to worldly possessions. Hear Jesus's words about salvation.

> MARK 10:27
> JESUS LOOKED AT THEM AND SAID, "FOR MORTALS IT IS IMPOSSIBLE, BUT NOT FOR GOD; FOR GOD ALL THINGS ARE POSSIBLE."

Salvation was the solution to our being out of alignment with God. As we apply our lives, being transformed by the Holy Spirit to the service of our neighbors' hunger, let's stop being cynical. In the face of Jesus's words telling us, there is no problem that cannot be handled by God, can we trust that whatever God calls us to do, we are capable of doing it with God's help? Jesus told us the poor and hungry will always be with us, and therefore, we can show them kindness whenever we want. I'm game for showing some kindness today. How about you?

In summary, guilt and cynicism are two important barriers to overcome if we are going to work alongside God in preparing the way for His kingdom. God will help us to overcome these. We do not work alone. God is with us, and we are also called alongside the entirety of Christ's body, the church. Let's get to work so we can all sit together under the vine and fig tree.

Reflection Questions

When am I placing guilt on my own conscience and not taking it to God in prayer?

Do I have 'conversations' with God, or are my prayers one-way?

Where does my motivation come from for seeking to do the things that Jesus commands us to do?

Why is it we sometimes fail to tie the gift of our spiritual hope and salvation to practical problems like ending hunger?

Do I too closely equate poor and hungry? Are we avoiding hungry people because they might always be poor?

Quadrilateralize

Scripture – How can we apply scripture about salvation to help defeat cynicism? How can we apply scripture to overcome guilt? How do we make sure to use scripture in context, to affirm our motivation to fulfill Jesus "Greatest Commandments"?

Tradition – How do the sacraments of the church inform our actions toward the hungry or suffering? What part of our corporate worship (as a group, or in a structured manner) aid in our ability to set aside cynicism and ward off the guilt that impedes our ability to serve others?

Experience – When have you felt guilt or cynicism, and how have you dealt with it? Has worship, prayer, relationships, or other parts of your faith helped you to move past it?

Reason – Why is it that we have these tools (like the means of grace) to defeat cynicism and guilt and yet we struggle with them? What are our next steps to overcome?

Chapter 4:

Behavior Change

Matthew 6:1-18
Luke 3:21 (Jesus prays after baptism)
Luke 5:16 (Jesus prays in the wilderness)
Luke 6:12 (Jesus prays all night before choosing disciples)
Matthew 14:23 (After the feeding of multitude)
Luke 9:18 (Jesus prays by himself)
John 17 (Jesus prays for God's will and the disciples)

We'll never end hunger by just feeding people
-REV. RAY BUCHANNAN

IN THE PREVIOUS CHAPTERS, WE'VE developed our understanding of the size and the scope of chronic hunger, we understand its relationship (as well as our relationship) with God, and we understand what we can do to make meaningful change through the means of grace. Still, I fear that understanding what to do next and doing it are two different things. Here is a similar example: I know a healthy balanced diet matched with exercise is essential to physical fitness, but for some reason, I don't seem to be able to avoid junk food or the couch. I recognize the value of eating healthy salads and taking brisk walks, but I'm not making the change very well. How do we get up-close and personal with the meaningful change to our behaviors that will help bring about an end to hunger? Like Paul says, "What I want to do, I do not do, but what I hate I do." (Romans 7:15)

The first thing we have to do is get excited about making a change. Tying emotion to what needs to be done is important. I think the term "zeal" might even apply to this area. It goes without saying; I should think that if you're truly passionate about something you will have energy to put behind a task or goal. The word zeal originally comes to us as a term for heat. Maybe that is the genesis of the term, "to light a fire under someone." Hunger isn't a topic where our primary response can remain lukewarm for long. A person's interest in remedying the intolerable scourge of hunger will either get extinguished or become full of the flames of passion. For those of us who are part of this Universal Church, I'm hoping we're the latter of the two.

I realize that what gives me energy might not pique the curiosity of someone else. With the stories we've shared in previous chapters, I've tried to charge up your eagerness to take the next step, but I'm not going to be able to hit on something that sparks fervor in all. Think about the Mud Cookies. We remember that it's frequently children who are the most impacted by hunger. Statistics say half of that 821 Million chronically malnourished are children and about 150 Million are under the age of 12. This is an appeal to the heart, and many people are motivated by matters of the heart to go to great heights of love.

Other folks find focus on solving problems with their heads more than their hearts. For these persons, we remember the numbers, statistics, and scale of protons, stars, and galaxies from Chapter 2. The detail-oriented people of the world and those who are motivated by the administrative, technical, and logistical challenges of hunger are just as capable of making an impact on hunger as those who are filled with heart-passion.

We also know that there are people who are motivated by their gut sense of right and wrong. These are the folks who are neither swayed by pitches to the head nor heart, but the gut. The "pit of your stomach" feeling people who are susceptible to shame, guilt, and cynicism. There is nothing like thinking about the excessiveness of a $1,000 meal to light a fire about hunger after the fact.

I also suspect that we each have all three types of motivation, but perhaps each person has a different balance. Regardless if you draw your zeal upon one or many, God gives us all the compassion to act.

Whatever brings you the zeal to end hunger, tap into that. True zeal for anything related to God's kingdom, if honest, is joined at the hip to charity and acts of mercy. But, being riled up means very little if there is no action, right? The recently coined term for being charged up and not taking any meaningful action is "slacktivism." (Slacker+Activism) If we want to see people upset about something, willing to rave like a lunatic and yet do nothing, we can find that on Twitter or Facebook, right? Our response as disciples of Christ needs to be something more. We need to ride the coattails of zeal and passion for forming habits that imitate Christ. Being excited about ending hunger and then not having a plan or a way to be engaged is like putting on a tuxedo without a formal event to attend. All dressed up and no ball. We need to know what to do when we're charged up with passion!

The human mind cannot maintain the fire of zeal without the discipline of chopping and stacking wood for that fire. When your heart, gut, or head is tugging you into action, we need to be ready. We need to have fuel for the fire. Preparing our lives and resources for Godly action is a form of discipleship that will require imitating Christ.

Our good intentions are also lost quickly when we're weighed down with decisions and choices. That is not to say that decisions and choices are a bad thing. Having lots of choices is often a great thing, just not when you're trying to get into a routine that will foster discipleship practices. Having some resources set aside, and a pre-made plan ready to be taken advantage of is essential.

Most importantly, I like to think that no matter what the immediate action is in front of us, we have to keep our goal in sight. Ensuring that 800+ million people are no longer hungry is a problem on a scale (as we discussed in chapter two) that is a bit large for most people. First, recognize that as Christians, Christ's call is sometimes at the level of His body, the church, and not at the level of an individual. Don't make your goal about ending global hunger all by yourself, but about what God is calling you specifically to do. You are one of many. At the very least, I believe each one of us can take responsibility for ending hunger for one other person in the developing world by combining Fasting, Prayer, and Giving. Remember, there are 2.2 billion Christians and only 821 million people who are chronically malnourished. Start with focusing on the one person that you can help right now, and let God bring you greater goals in time.

If you want an easy way to participate in a movement of individuals righting hunger by means of grace; check out FastPrayGive.org. Participation is simple and straight-forward, and can help you fast and pray to end hunger.

Preparations

First, get your bible and read Matthew chapter six. Dig into the first 18 verses. I would suggest reading it more than once. Here Jesus is giving us guidance on how to act, and it is important because it removes some decisions we have to make, and it follows up with some basic resources that we need to be effective.

Prayer

Prayer is not hard. I think a lot of people know this and still treat it as an Olympic sport. The excuse that prayer is hard and the incorrect belief that we must be great at praying is a deterrent. In the case of trying to end hunger, you can put all that at rest. Your prayer to end hunger can be simple and kept between you and God. There is no need for others to hear it or judge your praying abilities. Asking God to help you, help others, or just hear your concern for others…these are all very simple and reasonable prayers for hunger. If you still seek to ensure that you're saying the "right" thing, Jesus gave us a great example in Matthew chapter six.

Our Father in heaven,
Hallowed be your name.
Your kingdom come.
Your will be done,
on earth, as it is in heaven.
Give us this day our daily bread.
And forgive us our debts,
as we also have forgiven our debtors.
And do not bring us to the time of trial,
but rescue us from the evil one.

That makes it pretty easy, right? You see, there is even a part where we ask God to give us our daily bread. What does that mean? I think it means we're asking God for the food we need today to survive, **and** I think the "we" is not just for ourselves, but for all the people we hold in our heart. When you pray the Lord's prayer, imagine that the daily bread you are praying for is for you, your family, and the other people that God is asking you to help through discipleship. I have more to say about daily bread being more than about food, and is really we need each day spiritually, as well, to survive. However, that's another study. For now, just take way from this guidance that Christ gave us as a daily ritual, and to be about the things we need and not want.

I also have another way of helping you make this easy. Each week at FastPrayGive.org, we'll email a prayer that is specific to a call for God to be deeply involved in our efforts to end hunger. Even better, it will be based on a biblical passage you can read as well.

At the end of the day, prayer is a private time in which you can tell God anything. You most certainly don't have to only talk to God about hunger, or about problems. Jesus prayed to his "Father" (which was the most common way Jesus addressed God in prayer). It's how he addressed God at his baptism, in the wilderness, before inviting or selecting his disciples, before he fed the multitudes, in the temple, before he raised people from the dead, in the garden before he was arrested, and while on the cross. You can share anything you like with your heavenly father.

I like to suggest that you pray for global hunger while you are fasting. This affords you a great opportunity to tell God how it feels to be hungry, how it feels to have an empty stomach, how it feels to know a little portion of the life of a chronically malnourished person. You are given the gift to ask God for strength to abide in Him through a few hours of discomfort while you dedicate some resources to those in need.

While you're in this conversation with God, you also have an excellent opportunity to give praise and thanksgiving to God for all that you already have, and to pray for God to intercede on someone else's behalf. Feel free to lift up any of the concerns that you feel for God's presence to be known. A great way to wrap it up is to simply ask God to put **you** to work to end the suffering of others no matter what that looks like.

FASTING

Let us recall the quote in the introduction by Henri Nouwen about compassion. He said we needed to be weak with the weak, vulnerable

Behavior Change

with the vulnerable, and powerless with the powerless. It makes sense that at some level, full immersion in the human experience of hunger means we should be hungry with the hungry. Aside from all the other great reasons to make fasting a spiritual practice, I think we need to share the experience with those we seek to help. A well-defined and structured fast can rise to meet that objective.

The quickest way to quit doing anything is to have a bad experience doing it. So, there is some solid advice that I want to share a bit later, but first I think we need to talk about fasting. It seems like I hear about fasting more in relation to weight-loss or Jewish and Muslim tradition these days that Christian traditions. Why do you suppose that is?

Is it possible Jesus didn't sell it very well, unlike the prophets who came before Him? The times of Moses and Elijah saw the people of Israel in immense struggle and using fasting as an opportunity to find humility, show penitence, and display devotion. In Christ's time, the fast had become a drag imposed by religious leadership who liked to both fast and feast very openly to display their piety. This seems to be something of which Jesus was not a big fan. Remember Matthew chapter 6?

Don't get me wrong; Jesus was still in the camp that thought fasting was important. After all, he joined the ranks of Moses and Elijah by spending 40 days fasting at a time of tenuous transition and stress. In Matthew Chapter 6, Jesus did not say, "and *if* you fast…do it this way". He said, "and *when* you fast…do it this way." (paraphrase, emphasis added). Jesus assumes that of course, all of us should be fasting. Maybe that assumption has gotten lost on us over the years. I would have to think the loss of fasting as a key tenet of Christ's call to discipleship has led to the disproportion of feasting to fasting in our society.

Why are we recommending fasting as part of a movement to end hunger? There is a two-fold reason. First, mission-oriented activities like hunger-relief rely on our determination to live-out a promise to grow in faith. More simply put: Our mission as the church succeeds when fueled by discipleship. We need to be engaged in ways to strengthen our relationship with God. I know of no better way to strengthen a relationship than to invest in it with time and attention and self-sacrifice. Regular self-denial (sacrifice) and prayer are well known to make a difference in any disciple's life. As I stated in the first sentence of this section, though, we have to ease into fasting until it becomes comfortable. Otherwise, fasting is going to feel awkward and uncomfortable WAY more than it should.

The second reason for fasting is that we seem to live in a pie chart kind of world. Fasting, prayer, and giving are easily pushed off as something we don't usually have the resources to do in our daily lives and belonging only to special circumstances. "My pie chart is full and I have no extra time or money to give," people say. I say that is a bunch of hooey. The estimation that your pie-chart is "full" is an excuse and not a valid reason. God made your life's pie chart, to begin with, and can easily increase its capacity. The larger the pie the greater the number of slices, right?

Think of the parable of the servants and the talents in Matthew 25. God sees those who are working to build the kingdom and is willing to increase their capacity of the faithful to do additional good. Surely, we can begin, like the servants in that parable, to make some space on our own. By making time for fasting, you also make time to pray, because we're not spending the time we would have spent putting food into our mouths. Fasting also makes fiscal resources available for giving to end hunger, because we are saved the expense of eating during a fast. That's how *Fast* became the first word in FastPrayGive.

There are a few simple suggestions for fasting that will make this step of easing into it much easier. They are the FastPrayGive approach. They are not John Wesley's rules. However, if you want to research more about Wesley's fasting techniques and how they are derived from the Anglican practice, such research can also be of great value.

Fasting Suggestions

Be flexible. Consistency is awesome, but realizing that your fast should be a time of connecting between you and God, not stressful or strenuous.

Behavior Change

The fast should not force you to make awkward decisions or cancel dinner plans with friends and loved ones. Simply choose to fast a different meal, and plan ahead of time.

Skip a meal, not a series of meals. Wesley fasted from sundown on Thursday to 3:00 PM on Friday. Often, he added Wednesday and did the same. If you are into that, by all means, go for it, but we suggest that at first you take a more slimmed down approach and pick a single meal to fast.

Eat a good meal the mealtime directly prior to the fast. If you're going to fast lunch, eat a good breakfast.

Stick to a schedule. You'll find reward in being consistent. Try and fast the same meal every week. Claiming a meal as the one you "fasted" after you forgot to eat is defeating the purpose.

Don't go out of your way to fully avoid all temptation, but don't stare it down. Fasting is not a game of 'hide and go seek,' nor is it a game of endurance.

Drink adequate fluids during a fast. We can't recommend this enough. Drink adequate fluids.

Know when it's okay to skip fasting. If you're sick, you should probably eat, right? Let common sense be your guide. See the first suggestion about flexibility.

There are many among us who can't skip meals. People who are sick or have medical concerns. This doesn't mean you can't fast other things. consider giving up coffee or soda. Abstain from television or put your phone in a mode that limits you to the most basic features and eliminates distractions so that you might devote some time to being with God.

Giving

Generous people are people who take upon themselves the fate of the other.
- Emmanuel Levinas

There are so many books, studies, and websites devoted to teaching about generosity. They are too numerous to count. I just want to share a couple of real quick thoughts on how you might change your perception and in-turn your giving behavior.

If you look at the origins of the word *generous* you'll find that prior to the 18th century it meant you were of noble birth or of ideal character. We don't know why, but at some point the meaning shifted to describe a person who gave money or possessions to people who were in need.

Today we often think of generous as giving a large or significant sum of money or something of high value. Measuring generosity is an errand that can take considerable resources itself for little gain. I can argue that if generousity is really about making an impact on the person recieving a gift then measurement should lie within the realm of impact as well. The physical size of the gift is unimportant.

Jesus worked hard to share this value system through parables like the parable of the lost sheep, coin, and son (Luke Chapter 14). Jesus also directly told his disciples, while standing in the temple, that giving from abundance means far less than we think. (Luke 21:1-4)

Everything we have comes from God and belongs to God, and not just the leftovers. We can hear this guidance to change our behavior in two ways. First, give in response to a need, and not in response to our capacity to give. Second, give regardless of the size of the gift, no gift given from a call for compassion is too small.

FastPrayGive.org has, with this in mind, created a way for you to give a micro-donation each month to help people in need. We take these donations and provide grants to organizations who are responding to the needs of chronically malnourished people. Find out more at FastPrayGive.org

Reflection Questions

How does my perception of my ability to pray impact my willingness to pray or my dedication to daily prayer?

How often does your excitement lead to improved results in activities or tasks you are involved in? What techniques do you use to encourage excitement?

What things do others perceive as my 'causes' or things that I care dearly about? Would others say I have 'zeal' for these causes?

Quadrilateralize

Scripture – How does Jesus set an example of how we are to pray? Were Jesus' teachings on prayer more by example or by lessons taught (as in Matthew 6)?

Tradition – What parts of fasting and prayer do we inherit from our Jewish family? How have these traditions changed, and do we efficiently, adequately, or correctly carry out the traditions of the means of grace today? Which ones and how?

Experience – How has prayer been meaningful to you? Are there times when regular or intentional prayer has impacted your life? Are there times where you've had a positive experience with prayer or fasting?

Reason – Where does reason play into how we decide how to be engaged in prayer and fasting?

How do we arrive at the decision to do these works on a scale appropriate to ending hunger?

How do we use prayer and fasting to arrive at the decision to focus on our actions or individual contribution to a greater movement?

Chapter 5:

Casting a Vision

Matthew 22:36-40 (Jesus quotes Shema)
Matthew 28:16-20 (Jesus tells us where to go and what to do)

AT THE END OF THE previous chapter, I reminded you of a few motivating factors to stoke your zeal to end hunger. I also provided some concepts regarding fasting and prayer that could start your practice without too many distractions or decisions to lead you astray. The one necessary thing that I've not done is to cast a vision of what we hope to achieve as a FastPrayGive **movement**.

Two words, *end hunger*, have been uttered a lot in this study. The words themselves are much too vague to set you upon a path toward ending hunger without any idea on what the destination is supposed to look like. Obviously, there is no snap of fingers, the twinkle of a nose, or amazing machine that will end hunger instantaneously. It will take more people becoming active and involved in various ways for an extended period. What we must have is a movement of people with the force and motivation to stay involved. I believe that the larger body of people who will make up the movement are *Christian,* and the attractional motivation is *God through the means of grace.*

If ending hunger in our lifetime is a journey, and we want to get more people on the road, then we need to entice a potential traveler with what the destination looks like. I often think back to hiking in the Great Smoky Mountains National Park as a young adult, realizing that it's always easier to put one foot in front of the other when there was an awesome waterfall or vista at the end of the trail. You may have experienced similar feelings when the "pay-off" at the end of some task that requires great effort was worthy of the effort. If I hike a steep incline, for multiple hours, and all I get to see is the bald top of a mountain without a spectacular view, I might be disappointed. I don't think I'm alone in feeling cheated or demotivated if a reward doesn't live up to expectations. Keeping someone excited and energized to participate in an activity is essential in a sustained movement to end hunger.

Do we continually reward ourselves for work on behalf of people suffering from chronic hunger? That's not going to work either. We can adjust our expectations of *what* the pay-off is and *when* we receive it, in order to give us a sustaining encouragement. Helping others is a task that has a reward built-in, right? The act is in-itself the reward, and it becomes a self-rewarding virtuous cycle to continue the work. You see, the pay-off has to be part of the journey.

With regard to the needs of our human family (neighbors as Christ called them), we have to begin to recognize the benefits and rewards of the *means of grace* as we go along the trail. Hence the behavior change I've talked about in previous chapters. When we get this movement going, we'll celebrate both a daily connection with God *and* find the reward of improved relations with our creator as we seek to *end hunger* in the lives of our human family. God calls us to a journey of discipleship together with Him.

I want us to begin to see a vision of what change looks like, so I'll share it in what I think is its most basic form.

Vision: Millions of Christians focused on acts of spiritual growth as part of Christian discipleship while asking God to be deeply involved in their efforts to end hunger. All who are participating are listening to and following the Holy Spirit's guidance.

We will ***not*** end hunger via some missional campaign to fight chronic malnourishment. Turning churches into epicenters of hunger warriors will **not** work. We will end hunger when we make **more and better** disciples who create hope in others by making grace in the world.

You will notice that the intended vision does not include churches full of people devoting their whole lives to fight hunger or transforming churches into hunger relief agencies. Why? Because it's not the primary function of the church. The primary function of the church is "go and make of all disciples." This is important because FastPrayGive is about making more and better disciples that care about God's guidance and discipleship. The Holy Spirit will lead us to help end hunger. If we're to follow Jesus Christ, we must seek, as disciples, to care for the needs of those around us, provide for an end to suffering, all while preaching the good news. John Wesley liked to remind us that our faith was fulfilled by the good work we did, and that there were no truly good works without faith. Our faith is demonstrated by the times we have compassion, help others, and then share with all why we serve others.

Within the context of being Christian disciples who seek to end hunger, we want to choose the best tool that we can serve with, right? As the church, we have to choose the method that makes the most amount of sense: discipleship and disciple-building is our best tool. It's not only our best tool; it's our mission. Sharing our resources and support for organizations that disrupt hunger is a direction that I believe the Holy Spirit has in store for disciples of Jesus Christ.

You may have heard the term "asset-based community development." It's not a new idea, as it is based on a book written in 1993 which describes how a community's own assets and resources are the basis for ending what appears to be endless cycles of poverty. This is an idea that development can happen from the inside-out if resources are recognized, nurtured, and utilized inside the community in need. For instance, a successful implementation is where the community in need is listened to, nurtured, supported, and creates its own solution while the external influences are only engaged to assist with the requested support and resources.

In this example, communities that have been helped via resource provisioning are creating a lasting impact that is itself regenerative, independent, and kick-started by neighbors and *not* directed by the groups providing the resources. The key word here is *impact*.

What has been revealed to me over time is that if we reclaim the Christian method of discipleship to impact our own lives through spiritual disciplines like **prayer, fasting, and generous giving** we can make a new generation of disciples who can have staying power in the long fight of enabling communities to self-heal. We will do this by providing resources and supporting efforts that result in real impact. We share the good news about why we're helping and move on to help the next neighbors in need.

The Change

We have to stop splitting our focus. If a large swathe of Christians continue to think it's our church's first job to fix the suffering of the world instead of making disciples we're going to fail at both. There are some hairs to be split here. Can the church contribute and be part of the hunger solution? Yes. Can the church be accountable and responsible for the entire solution? No. Can Christians play a role in being accountable and responsible? Absolutely. I see well-formed Christians being involved in every aspect. But the church as a body would be better suited to play a role of consultation when it comes to solutions, and direct resources and energy where they are needed, while wholly focused on making disciples for Jesus Christ.

Disciples who ask God for guidance will receive and respond to the direction of the Holy Spirit. The sum of the actions of many disciples gives a church direction. Those disciples become thought leaders inside the congregational body and speak with a prophetic voice to their church. A church can feel confident in what it is doing if it's being led by healthy and well-formed disciples. A church cannot know what it is supposed to do tomorrow unless its leaders are asking God, "What is next, and will You help us God?"

Inside our human family, our churches should seek out the brokenness of one another. We bind up our wounds and love one another. We strengthen our relationship with God and trust in God as we worship, pray, have fellowship, and celebrate the sacraments. In turn, we create disciples who are more balanced in their place in society, navigating the world around them regardless of the peril. A heightened awareness of injustice and suffering is undergirded by a preparedness to organize and reject the spiritual forces of wickedness. You may have said this last phrase as part of your baptismal or confirmation vows.

Spiritually well (healthy) disciples make more disciples. The spiritually well disciple sees God in everything, observes injustice with greater clarity, moves in concert with God's action, and has a stronger prophetic voice. These are the people who can create the spiritual and economic capital needed to develop the assets already present in communities the world over, sharing resources that are abundant elsewhere. Well-formed disciples create *impact*.

The Engagement Dichotomy

It is a reasonably held belief that if we're more engaged with a mission, knowing fully who we're helping, communicating with them directly, and building a tight and interlocked community with those in need, we will find success in mission and ministry. I have held that belief for a long time.

What I failed to do, however, was to consider what it meant to succeed in mission and ministry. Success is measured against a stated goal. But which goal are we trying to achieve? Success in the mission field is not mutually exclusive to success in ministry, but do mission and ministry have the same goals?

I've heard people talk about churches being a "great commission" church versus a "great commandment" church. What does that even mean? I think it's a response to a deeply held conviction that some congregations see their primary purpose as missional, meant to follow the great commandment of Christ to love God and love neighbor (Matthew 22) – and some congregations see their purpose as a church is to follow the great commission and make disciples of Jesus (Matthew 28). I doubt there are many churches which see themselves as one and not the another. There is a good possibility that some congregations might identify more with one operating framework then the other. It might also depend on who you ask in church leadership.

I'm a Methodist and am part of a global headcount of about 40 million people who belong to churches with roots in the teaching of John and Charles Wesley (and others). Specifically, I'm part of The United Methodist Church, which has about 12.7 million people globally in our membership. This is the faith organization who has shaped my view, and I'm going to reference some of it in the following paragraph. If you're not part of a Methodist church, I hope you'll hear our polity and discipline as guidance and not theology. For our theology, we reference Holy Scripture. As of this writing, the mission statement of the United Methodist Church (UMC) is to make disciples of Jesus Christ **for the** transformation of the world. (*See The Book of Discipline of the United Methodist Church 2016;* paragraph 120) Note it says, 'for the' and not 'and the.' They are not to be done in successive order, but concurrently. It also doesn't say the UMC will transform the world **by** making Disciples for Jesus Christ, because once we make disciples, the work has to continue. The disciples must go and lead in the transformation of the world. You may remember our discussion of grace early in this study when we talked about Justifying versus Sanctifying grace. A disciple is born through Justifying grace and then goes on to transform the world through sanctification by the means of grace. See how it all ties together? The fulfillment of the Great Commission to make disciples leads to the grace-filled transformation of the world through the Great Commandment to love God and neighbor.

I'm not making this stuff up. At your leisure, check out *The Book of Discipline of the United Methodist Church 2016* paragraph 121, where the commissioning of disciples and the command that we love our neighbors are clearly stated as part of the foundation for our mission. Want more? Check out paragraph 122 and read the process by which we're to carry out this mission. I'm merely re-hashing what was written by a large group of people who prayed and asked God for guidance on how to move a large group of people in mission.

Disciple Creation and Missional Impact by loving God and neighbor are intertwined. Without healthy and replicating disciples, there is no energy in our mission. Not only do we need more and better disciples to build upon tradition and experience by loving and caring for our neighbors, but worship and devotion are hollow without disciplined actions on behalf of compassion and justice. We can't preach and share the gospel in a space devoid of demonstrable love and caring. On top of that, if we aren't making new disciples every day, who is going to carry forward our work? Who?

What I am trying to communicate is that FastPrayGive provides a set of actions that help us focus less on being engaged with persons in need and more with God. Because we seek to connect with God, we can align our goals with God's to make disciples by loving and serving others. We'll often pause and listen to what God calls us to do next. We may yet still hear a renewed cry to build a closer relationship with those in need. For certain, when we use the means of grace to step back and evaluate our progress, our goals, and success, the process becomes a living and breathing cycle.

What do I see?

I can't see into the future and give you an accurate vision of what FastPrayGive will look like ten years from now. I wish I could. It might save me some difficult decisions. I hope it looks like an organically grown, true grassroots movement of sacrificial discipleship leading to personal action against hunger.

Every person currently participating in FastPrayGive is fasting, praying, and giving a micro-donation ($8-12) each month to alleviate hunger. Today we're in our early hours of existence. I see modest growth of around a few dozen new subscribers each month. Growth by word of mouth and introduction occurs largely from advocates that can speak to the means of grace or have participated with our partner organizations like Rise Against Hunger, who are extremely successful in fostering and measuring impact in the fight against hunger. These early adopters are activists. They know that God must be deeply involved to change our church and world. These are the grassroots participants we need!

How, do you ask, do we accomplish this? We invite them to join us. By working with our partners, like Rise Against Hunger, we bring fun and exciting meal packaging events to those churches via matching grants. This allows us to put resources into the hands of our partners, fighting the root causes of hunger and tell more people about FastPrayGive while faithfully disbursing the monthly donations.

On the day we grow to a few thousand participants who ascribe to the concept that fasting one meal, praying for the end of world hunger, and giving the cost of their meal to achieve that goal, there will be hundreds of people praying each day around any given mealtime for people in need. Small groups like Sunday School classes, Home meetings, bands, and covenant groups, might make FastPrayGive part of their bond with one another and whole churches may take up a challenge to Fast, Pray, and Give at increasing percentages.

The next ring outward in our movement will come into existence when the incremental growth in revenue and support to our partners becomes something they have to report to their donors, stakeholders, and board of directors. At that point, the messaging grows to a point where controlling it is difficult, other than to share the narrative that Christian love is focused on ending world hunger. The idea that the means of grace and discipleship creation is an instigator of behavior change and can impact those who are chronically malnourished is infectious. We now have a story of growth and promise to tell.

This whole idea started with a vision of the 40 million people whose churches are part of the World Methodist Council. If ten percent of those 40 million people participated (4 million) and donated as little as $8 per month, we would have $32 Million dollars each month to bless the work of partners who are *ending hunger on a daily basis*. More importantly, we would have millions of people enacting a behavioral change in their lives. They would be asking God, "Please be deeply involved in my efforts to be a better disciple. What Lord, do you want me to do?" They would be enacting *means of grace*, which was, and still is, a pillar of the Methodist movement. After all, God created us, loves us, and promises to do so indefinitely through our interaction with his Son Jesus Christ. "As you have done it to the least of these, my brothers and sisters, you have done it to me."

Will you join me today? Subscribe at FastPrayGive.org and **fast** one meal per week, **pray** during that time for God to help us *end hunger*, and **give** to make an impact in the lives of those in need. Oh, and if you're already participating, be sure to share it with your friends on social media at *@FastPrayGive* on Facebook, Instagram, and Twitter.

Reflection Questions

Does that body of faith that I belong to identify as a Matthew 28 or Matthew 22 church?

Do I expect a tangible reward for everything I do, including helping others?

Does your congregation have thought leaders who speak with a prophetic voice?

Quadrilateralize

Scripture – How has Jesus's teaching in Matthew 22 and 28 set the trajectory of our spiritual lives? Do you feel these scriptural references are an instructional or simply historical reference?

Tradition – Before John Wesley, Jacob Albright and others documented a missional strategy of the Methodist movement, how did God's covenants with Abraham, The Israelites in Exodus, and the other prophets inform our understanding of Christ's teachings?

Experience – How has a sense of satisfaction for a job well done, a feeling of warmth in your relationship with God, or a feeling of oneness in your church's vision impacted your understanding of our theological task?

Reason – What stops our congregations, denominations, and faith bodies from adopting a "God-sized" vision of nearly every church member being an active disciple whom regularly asks God, "What do you want me to do?"

Casting a Vision

www.ingramcontent.com/pod-product-compliance
Lightning Source LLC
Chambersburg PA
CBHW071035080526
44587CB00015B/2626